Postcards from

The Russian Revolution

Introduction by
Andrew Roberts

The publisher would like to thank the following for their assistance in producing this book: Irina Baysheva for translating the Russian, John Fraser, John Pinfold and Ian Shapiro.

First published in 2008 by the Bodleian Library
Broad Street
Oxford OX1 3BG

www.bodleianbookshop.co.uk

ISBN: 1 85124 386 0
ISBN 13: 978 1 85124 386 0

Introduction © Andrew Roberts, 2008
This edition © Bodleian Library, University of Oxford, 2008

'Events in Poland, June 1905' and 'In his Fear to Save Himself from Danger, his is Running to his Ruin' by André Félix Ruberty 1877–1963 © ADAGP, Paris and DACS, London 2008.

'Governor's House, Tobolsk' reproduced by kind permission of the Ian Shapiro Collection and does not form part of John Fraser's collection.

Designed by Dot Little
Printed and bound in China by C&C Offset Printing Co. Ltd.
British Library Catalogue in Publishing Data
A CIP record of this publication is available from the British Library

Collector's Foreword

From an early age I was interested in history. My mother gave me my first postcard, of King George VI at his coronation. When she took me to St Paul's Cathedral, I bought a postcard of Nelson's statue. In 1944 my local Woolworths sold sepia photographic postcards of generals Eisenhower, Alexander, and Montgomery. From then on I was a compulsive collector of any postcards of a historical or current political interest.

I was strongly influenced by the example of my artist aunt, Helen McKie (pronounced to rhyme with key). She had a large collection of postcards, mainly of views, arranged in order of country and subject matter, which she used for reference purposes. So I had her example to follow, and after her death I acquired her postcards of Hitler (she was the first woman artist to be allowed in the Brown House when she was commissioned to do a series on Germany in 1932 for the *Sketch*) and also cards of Rome with its Fascist décor. (There is an entry for her in *Who Was Who* for the 1950s.)

John Fraser, London

Introduction

The postcard was the early twentieth century's equivalent of today's email: written and sent quickly, they often expressed a single thought and were not intended to be a lasting contribution to literature. Yet, as this very remarkable collection of postcards from the Russian Revolution – or in fact Revolutions – shows, they are of great historical and social interest. Moreover, postcards can also be a profound artistic medium as well as projecting powerful political propaganda. At their best they can recreate the immediacy, excitement and emotion of great historical events, which is certainly what this collection achieves for the 1905, the (February 1917) Kerensky, and the (October 1917) Bolshevik Revolutions in Russia.

The postcards in this attractive short book represent only a small fraction of a vast collection of thousands acquired by the Bodleian Library from a single individual, John Fraser, who amassed it over a period of six decades, ever since he was a schoolboy. The immensely broad nature of the collector's interests, as well as his ability to amass so many cards of such high individual quality, is also celebrated by this volume.

The depiction of Tsar Nicholas II as an autocrat and tyrant, indeed a 'Man of Blood', might seem strange to those of us more used to his image as a pacific personality, weak-minded monarch and loving husband and father, but it can be seen in the propaganda postcards from both the 1905 and the 1917 Revolutions. The murder of the Tsar and his family and servants in July 1918 – shot and bayoneted to death in the basement of the Ipatiev House in Ekaterinburg before their corpses were flung down a mineshaft – is eerily foreshadowed in French postcards from the 1905 period depicting the assassination of the Tsar's uncle, the Grand Duke Sergei Aleksandrovich. Meanwhile, Father George Gapon, the Orthodox priest who organized the march on St Petersburg's Winter Palace in January 1905, the violent repression of which on 'Bloody Sunday' sparked the attempted Revolution, is presented as an almost Christ-like figure.

The demands for a free Russia – 'Russie Libre' – depicted on some of the French postcards have their own irony by 1922 when V.I. Lenin, Leon Trotsky and Joseph Stalin – depicted here in charming informal poses – extended their grasp on power after their victory in the

Russian Civil War. In the course of that conflict terrible famines broke out, from deliberate political as well as natural causes, which are also depicted in this collection.

Why should anyone wish to print, buy or send a postcard of bread queues full of starving Ukrainian women and children, one might wonder? Because postcards had a political dimension to them, with an element of reportage as important as the mere reproduction of iconic images. As well as being like emails they were the pre-radio, pre-television equivalent of a news bulletin from abroad.

For all that many made fairly crude political statements for or against Tsarism, the Mensheviks, the Bolsheviks, etc., on occasion these postcards could depict hauntingly beautiful imagery. Before the deadening onset of the Socialist Realism movement under Stalin – full of sturdy, handsome peasant women driving tractors towards the New Dawn - there was a resurgence of fine Russian drawing and painting that is well represented here. Just as Satan is reputed to have all the best tunes, so the posters and postcards of the early Bolshevik movement produced some of the finest political art ever created. It was propaganda for a monstrous tyranny, of course, but it was strong, captivating, and well drawn.

Maxim Gorky, Leo Tolstoy, Catherine Breshkovsky ('the mother of the Revolution'), Alexander Kerensky, Lenin in close-up, a jolly, pipe-smoking Stalin, and many other identifiable individuals are all depicted, either in photographic or drawing or cartoon form, but so is an elderly, white-bearded man who turns out to be Almighty God himself, as satirized by the anti-religious Soviet propaganda machine. The sheer comprehensiveness of the collection, and lack of political bias in the choice of what was amassed, makes this remarkable and attractive volume a fascinating visual snapshot of political events in Russia from the Russo-Japanese War of 1904–5 right up to the Bolshevik victory in the Civil War seventeen years later.

Andrew Roberts

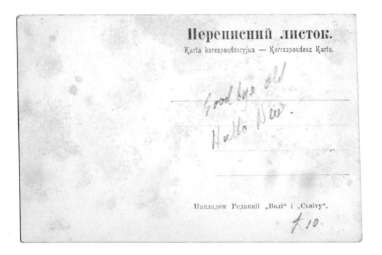

Social Democracy and Autocracy

Jointly published by *Liberty* and *Light*, the message of this
undated cartoon is clear. The boat of 'Social democracy'
is successfully navigating the rocks and is pulling strongly
towards the light of the promised new dawn, whilst
'Autocracy', weighed down by plutocrats, officials and the
Church, is breaking up on the rocks.

Соціяльна демократія і самодержавіє.

ОТКРЫТОЕ ПИСЬМО.
CARTE-POSTALE.

The Poster of The First Russian Revolution

<<Land and Freedom>>

135

№799

Land and Freedom

This postcard uses the slogan of the Narodniks (the People's Will Party, who saw the peasantry as the vanguard of the Revolution) to provide an emotive image of the first Russian Revolution in 1905.

Twenty years later, in a speech to the Second Congress of the Society of Political Prisoners and Deportees, Trotsky wrote:

'1905 would clarify the slogan "Land and Freedom". It was called romantic and fantastical, and indeed there was in it a little romance, but this slogan, throwing off its romantic skin, turned into the iron reality of the confiscation of the landlord's property and the abolition of the nobility who had oppressed Russia for centuries.'

9

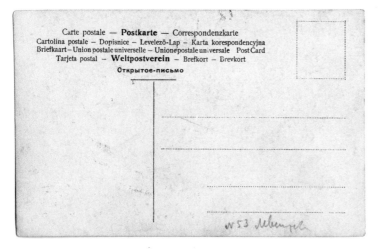

Untitled

This striking example of early revolutionary art shows
a crowd of workers and peasants joyously acclaiming
the figure of Liberty, who stands before a funerary
monument to Karl Marx. The slogan on the banner reads
'Freedom, Equality, Brotherhood', whilst the inscription at
the base of the tribune reads 'Mankind'.

Father Gapon. The Revolutionary Outbreak in St. Petersburg.

This English postcard dates from the time of the first Russian Revolution in 1905.

George Gapon (1870–1906) was a Russian Orthodox priest and a popular working-class leader who organized the Assembly of Russian Factory and Mill Workers of St Petersburg. The movement's objectives were both to defend workers' rights and to elevate their moral and religious outlook. Unknown to the vast majority of the members, however, was the fact that the Assembly was sponsored by the police and the Tsarist secret police, the Okhrana. Nevertheless, Gapon was not simply a secret police agent as he also had aims of his own.

Following Bloody Sunday, Gapon fled abroad, first to Switzerland and then to London. He returned to Russia in October, but was hanged by some of his former comrades in the Socialist Revolutionary Party when they realized he had been an agent provocateur.

Father Gapon.

No. 1 THE REVOLUTIONARY OUTBREAK IN St. PETERSBURG.   *By permission of the Proprietors of the Sphere.*   [*Copyright.*

13

PICTORIAL POST CARD.

This space may only be used for Inland Postage.

The Address only to be written here.

Rail Photo Series, LANCASTER & Co., Tunbridge Wells

Is this before the Mansion House 4th February? I am looking for Max & but cannot find him B.6.

W. Max Ettlinger 906 Grosvenor Rd Canonbury 8

The Revolutionary Outbreak in St. Petersburg

This English card was posted on 3 February 1905, just days after the outbreak of the first Russian Revolution, and the massacre on Bloody Sunday (22 January). It captures something of the resolve, and also of the optimism, of the demonstrators before they were fired on by Tsarist troops.

No. 3. THE REVOLUTIONARY OUTBREAK IN St. PETERSBURG. *By permission of the Proprietors of the Sphere.* [*Copyright.*

15

Karta Korespondencyjna.
Postkarte. — Union Postale Universelle.

Strzelanie do ludu dnia 22. Stycznia
1905-r. w Petersburgu.

Ilustrowane karty korespondencyjne „Naprzodu".

Untitled

This dramatic view dates from 1905 and depicts Bloody Sunday, 22 January 1905, when unarmed peaceful demonstrators, who were marching to present a petition to the Tsar, were gunned down by troops in front of the Winter Palace in St Petersburg. It is thought that around 1,000 people were killed or wounded. Although the Tsar himself was not present, he was blamed for the massacre, and the incident unquestionably undermined support for his government.

The protest march was led by Father Gapon, who was in the pay of the secret police and who had been warned not to proceed with the march, but decided to go ahead anyway. He himself was uninjured, although many of those around him were killed.

Rose
13/X 1906.

17

The Death of the Grand Duke Sergei

This French cartoon dates from February 1905. The figure of the Revolution is holding up the head of the assassinated Grand Duke, whilst Nicholas II cowers in the background, awaiting his turn. The caption reads, 'Bow down, Nicholas, it is the turn of the Revolution'.

The Grand Duke Sergei (1857–1905) was a younger brother of Alexander III and uncle to Nicholas II. He was appointed Governor General of Moscow in 1891 and as commander of the Moscow military district in 1896.

He was killed by a bomb thrown at him by Ivan Kalyayev, a member of the Socialist Revolutionary Party, on 17 February 1905.

The artist who drew this cartoon, Orens Bonaventure Charles Denizard (he usually signed himself as simply 'Orens'), was born in 1879. He was one of the most prolific of the postcard cartoonists of the time, producing an almost weekly comment on events from around 1902 to 1908, many of them in numbered series.

L'A.S.- N°7 - N°l°(- N° 150 - F.S. cutoris
Et Mort du Grand Duc
- Serge -
(17 février 1905)
« — Baise toi Nicolas, c'est
la Révolution qui fait
ta ronde »

19

Untitled

A French cartoon, which dates from the time of the 1905 Revolution. The autocrat Nicholas II is hanging from the gibbet, whilst the revolutionary crowd acclaim the event. Note the French cap of liberty above the banner.

Nicholas's boots, which have fallen off, are labelled Poland and Finland. These refer to the movements for national liberation in those countries at the time of the Revolution, which attracted widespread sympathy in France.

The artist of this cartoon was Mille, who, like Orens, was a leading political cartoonist of the time.

NICOLAS II
L'AUTOCRATE

FINLANDE

21

Events in Poland, June 1905

This French cartoon refers to the crushing of the nationalist movements in Poland in 1905. Since the eighteenth century the French had had considerable sympathy for Poland, and Napoleon's establishment of the Grand Duchy of Warsaw was still remembered in both countries. This cartoon was intended to reflect that sympathy and also to act as a warning. Whilst Nicholas tramples the Poles underfoot and says, 'Well then, all roads lead to Rome …', the Voice of France responds 'take care … to the guillotine also (see Louis XVI)'.

This linking of Nicholas's possible fate to that which had befallen Louis XVI (and also Charles I of England) was a constant theme of cartoons and postcards of the time.

Événements de Pologne - Juin 1905 -
Le Czar: Eh aïe donc !... Tout chemin mène à Rome...
La voix de la France { Prends garde... à la Guillotine aussi!
(Voir Louis XVI)

The Sovereign People Advancing, 1905

This French cartoon is by Orens and dates from
November 1905. A Russian peasant advances, holding the
arms of Nicholas II – a head severed by the guillotine.
The two heads rising out of the shield represent Poland
and Finland (victims of Nicholas's tyranny) whilst the
arms at the bottom hold the torch of liberty and the
scales of justice. The comment above reads, 'Tyrants, pay
your debts.'

LES ARMOIRIES DE NICOLAS II
N° 4

TYRANS PAYEZ
VOS DETTES

FINLANDE

F. JACK. é. PARIS.

AUX. TYRANS

LIBERTÉ

LE PEUPLE
SOUVERAIN
S'AVANCE.
1905

Orens. 05.

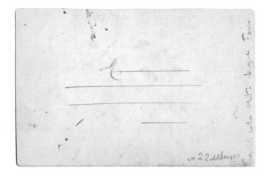

In his Fear to Save Himself from Danger, he is Running to his Ruin

This French cartoon dates from 1905. It portrays Nicholas II fleeing from the revolutionary outbreak amongst the sailors of the Black Sea Fleet (later to be immortalized in Eisenstein's film *Battleship Potemkin*), but in his fear he does not see that he is about to fall into the 'Abyss of Brutal Repression'.

ODESSA JUIN 1905

Nº 8

Abîme de la répression brutale

Dans sa frayeur pour se sauver du danger, il court à sa perte...

Открытое письмо.—Carte Postale.
ВСЕМІРНЫЙ ПОЧТОВЫЙ СОЮЗЪ. РОССІЯ

Мѣсто для корреспонденціи   Адресъ.

Господину

11   ИЗДАНІЕ „LUMO" МОСКВА.

Moscow. Barricade and Ruins at Grousiny

This classic view of a street barricade dates from the 1905 Revolution, when many working-class suburbs of Moscow rose in revolt and blockaded streets, sometimes in conscious emulation of the Paris Commune of 1871. The 1905 Revolution also saw the first appearance of workers' councils or soviets. There was later fierce fighting in the streets of Moscow as the authorities sought to regain control.

The large signboard on top of the barricade has been taken from a local sauna.

МОСКВА в баррикадах и развалинах. | barricad et ruines a MOSCOU
Грузины баррик. в Тишинском. п. | Grousiny. Pichinsky per.

29

ОТКРЫТОЕ ПИСЬМО.

Мѣсто
для
марки.

The Prime Minister in the Role of Saviour of Russia. Forward to the Light!

This ironic postcard showing the Prime Minister (almost certainly Sergei Witte) trampling on the people dates from the period when Witte was brought back into the government to help deal with the civil unrest that followed Bloody Sunday in 1905. The banner he is carrying reads 'All Love Freedom!'.

ДА ЗДРАВСТВУЕТЪ СВОБОДА!

Премьеръ-министръ — въ роли
спасителя Россіи. —

ВПЕРЕДЪ!!
Къ ...... свѣту!!

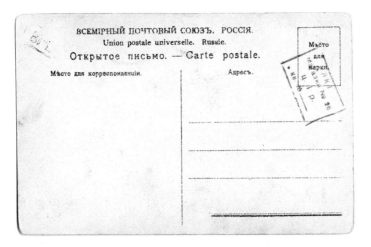

Golovin Gives his Answer to Stolypin

This complex cartoon dates from 1907, when the Prime Minister, Stolypin, was seeking to dissolve the Duma, of which Golovin was the Chairman. Whilst Golovin and his colleagues argue with Stolypin over the fate of the Duma, the plutocrats laugh and crowds of workers and peasants gather in the background, seemingly ready to sweep away both the Liberal Cadets, of whom Golovin was one, and the forces of autocracy.

In the event, Stolypin was able to dissolve the Duma without facing any serious unrest in the country. He remained Prime Minister until 1911, when he was assassinated whilst attending the opera in Kiev.

ГОЛОВИНЪ ПИШЕТЪ ОТВѢТЪ СТОЛЫПИНУ.

Направо—Ѳ. А. Головинъ съ I. В. Гессеномъ. За столомъ, сбросивъ министерскій мундиръ, сидятъ г. Кутлеръ; рядомъ съ нимъ депутаты Кизеветтеръ и Нечитайло; за его спиною—г. Алексинскій. Въ бурѣ—товарищъ предсѣдателя г. Познанскій. Среди другихъ—депутатъ Пьяныхъ и проч.

His Imperial Majesty Sovereign Emperor Nikolai Alekseevich

This view was clearly intended to show Nicholas as the successful huntsman about to plunge his dagger into the stag he has shot, but it has a staged, uneasy, feel to it, with the luggage label marked 'N' suggesting that perhaps the stag has been specially chosen for the Emperor. Note the sprigs of oak leaves carefully placed around the antlers and between the legs of the stag.

Его Императорское Величество Государь
Императоръ Николай Александровичъ.

The Children of His Majesty the Emperor

This card dates from 1908 and shows the children
wearing the sailor suits that were fashionable at the time.
From left to right Marie (b.1899), Anastasia (b.1901),
Alexei (b.1904), Olga (b.1895), Tatiana (b.1897).

In this picture the Tsarevich appears the picture of health,
with no sign of the haemophilia which was said to plague
him in later years and which enabled Rasputin to extend
his influence over the Tsarina.

АВГУСТЕЙШІЕ ДѢТИ Е.И.В. ГОСУДАРЯ ИМПЕРАТОРА

Untitled

This undated card depicts the children of Nicholas and Alexandra a few years before their murder in Ekaterinburg.

With the benefit of hindsight, the haunted look in the children's eyes seems to suggest a foreknowledge of the terrible fate that awaited them.

1613–1913 Tercentenary Jubilee of the House of Romanov

In 1913 the Romanov dynasty celebrated its tercentenary. The festivities began on 21 February with a grand service of thanksgiving in the Kazan Cathedral in St Petersburg, which was followed by four days of receptions, balls, and a gala performance of Glinka's opera *A Life for the Tsar* at the Mariinsky Theatre. Nicholas wrote in his diary, 'Thank Lord God who shed his grace upon Russia and us all so that we could decently and joyously celebrate the days of the tercentenary of the Romanovs' accession'. Others were less enthusiastic and noted the thin crowds watching the processions, as well as Rasputin's participation in the proceedings.

Later, in May, the royal family made a two-week tour of historic Russian towns, retracing the route taken by Michael Romanov on his way to the throne three centuries before. Once again there was a marked lack of public enthusiasm, one observer noting that 'There was nothing in the feeling of the crowd but shallow curiosity.' The celebrations reached their climax in Moscow, where there was a further four-day programme of receptions, banquets, and church services. It is no wonder that by the final day the Tsar was recording in his diary 'Finally I sat on my feet because of tiredness.'

Amongst the places visited by the royal family on their tour was the Ipatiev Monastery near Kostroma, which was where Michael Romanov had agreed to accept the throne in 1613. They cannot have guessed that both their own lives and the dynasty itself would come to an end in the Ipatiev House in Ekaterinburg only five years later.

This postcard from the time of the tercentenary depicts the whole line of Romanov rulers from Tsar Michael (1613–45) through to Nicholas and Alexandra and the Tsarevich Alexei.

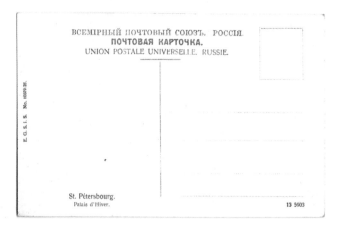

ВСЕМІРНЫЙ ПОЧТОВЫЙ СОЮЗЪ. РОССІЯ.
ПОЧТОВАЯ КАРТОЧКА.
UNION POSTALE UNIVERSELLE. RUSSIE.

E.G.S.i.S. No. 10509-25.

St. Pétersbourg.
Palais d'Hiver.

13 5903

St Petersburg. The Winter Palace

A pre-First World War view. The storming of the Winter Palace in October 1917 was to become a central part of the Bolshevik myth of the Revolution, and it forms the climax of Eisenstein's film *October*, which was made to commemorate the tenth anniversary of the Revolution. These scenes in the film were shot in the palace itself and they have a documentary quality about them that has misled many people into thinking they are an accurate portrayal of events that night. In reality the Winter Palace was barely defended and the takeover by the Bolsheviks was largely without bloodshed; more people were injured in the making of the film than in the actual assault on the palace. Nevertheless, the capture by the Bolsheviks of this symbol of governmental power and authority undoubtedly marked their accession to power, however temporary it may have seemed initially both to their opponents and to themselves.

С.-Петербургъ.
Зимній Дворецъ.

43

ВСЕМІРНЫЙ ПОЧТОВЫЙ СОЮЗЪ. РОССІЯ.
ПОЧТОВАЯ КАРТОЧКА.
UNION POSTALE UNIVERSELLE. RUSSIE.

E. O. S. i. S. No. 10716/21.

Pétrograde.
Place Marinsky et L'ambassade Allemande.

14 53641

Petrograd. The German Embassy and Mariinsky Square

St Petersburg was renamed Petrograd during the First World War as the city's name was perceived as being too German. In the immediate aftermath of the February Revolution in 1917 the Provisional Government used the Mariinsky Palace as its headquarters.

The equestrian statue is a monument to Tsar Nicholas I. It dates from the 1850s and is notable for balancing on just two of the horse's legs.

Петроградъ.   Германское посольство и Маріинская площадь.

Military 5½% Loan. Are you going to help our glorious army fight the enemy? Have you participated in the military loan?

The Tsarist government was unprepared for the scale or the cost of the First World War and in 1916 was compelled to issue a 5½% military loan to help finance the war. A series of posters and postcards were produced to encourage people to donate their savings to the war effort.

On the back of the card is a patriotic slogan, 'The enemy must be broken. Until then there can be no peace. Remember these words and take part in the preparation for victory by subscribing to the military loan'.

The designer of this card was Sigismund Vidberg (b.1890).

Помогаете ли Вы
доблестной арміи
сражаться съ
врагомъ?

Приняли ли Вы
участіе въ займѣ?

ВОЕННЫЙ 5½ % ЗАЕМЪ

Изданіе Управленія по дѣламъ мелкаго кредита. *Складъ изданія*
въ редакціи „Вѣстникъ мелкаго кредита", Петроградъ, Ивановская, 13.

Эксп. Заг. Гос. Бум.

ВСЕМІРНЫЙ ПОЧТОВЫЙ СОЮЗЪ. РОССІЯ.
UNION POSTALE UNIVERSELLE. RUSSIE.

ПОЧТОВАЯ КАРТОЧКА. — CARTE POSTALE.

5½% Military Loan. Our glorious army bleeding for the motherland is fulfilling its duty. You also can fulfil your duty by subscribing to the loan.

Another patriotic postcard seeking to mobilize support on the home front for the increasingly unpopular war. This card was sent from Petrograd to Sebastopol in December 1916, and the sender reveals that he himself is about to leave for the front.

ВОЕННЫЙ
5½% ЗАЕМЪ.

Наше доблестное воинство,
проливая кровь за родину,
свято исполняетъ свой
долгъ.

Исполните и Вы свой — подпишитесь на заемъ.

Изданіе Управленія по дѣламъ мелкаго кредита.
Складъ изданія въ редакціи „Вѣстникъ мелкаго кредита", Петроградъ, Ивановская, 13.

Эксп. Заг. Гос. Бум.

Military 5½% Loan

The slogan on the back of this card reads, 'The soldiers at the front are dauntlessly holding the line against the enemy. Take part in this united action and subscribe to the loan.'

This particular card is of historic importance as it was written only a day after the Tsar's abdication. The dates are all 'old style' and the text reads:

'4 March

'Today we have learned that our Emperor has abdicated from the throne. On the night of 2–3 March Goutskov [Guchkov] and Choulguin [Shulgin] went to Pskov on behalf of the council of the Duma to submit the wish of the Provisional Government to him. He signed a paper which had already been prepared.'

ВОЄННЫЙ
5⅒⅘ ЗАЄМЪ

Handwritten on postcard: British Submarines' crews' Russian Parent-ship Reval March 1917

British Submarines' Crews and Russian Parent Ship, Reval, March 1917

It is now almost totally forgotten that a British submarine flotilla operated in the Baltic between 1915 and 1918, where they were attached to the Russian Baltic Fleet at Reval (now Tallinn).

The force comprised six E-class submarines and five of the smaller C-class. The E-class boats, with one exception, reached the Baltic by slipping undetected through the Danish Straits in water only ten metres deep. The C-class boats made a longer journey via Archangel and the White Sea Canal. Both classes of boats operated successfully in the Baltic, intercepting German shipping and sinking at least one German warship.

In 1918 the German occupation of Reval and the Brest-Litovsk peace treaty between Russia and Germany forced the remaining British submarines to move to Helsinki, where they were subsequently scuttled to prevent them falling into enemy hands.

This was not the end of British naval operations in the Baltic. In 1919 a force under Admiral Cowan supported the Estonians in their fight for independence, attacking the Russian navy's main base at Kronstad and destroying the Red Navy as an effective fighting force.

Untitled

This postcard, produced by the A.F. Postnov factory in Moscow, dates from the immediate aftermath of the February Revolution and the overthrow of the Tsar. The caption reads 'Now I see what the imperial throne is. A fright that we shivered with fear. Why have we fed this damned flock of Ravens with our blood?'. The dead ravens at the foot of the overturned throne bear the names of some of the most hated Tsarist ministers and officials – Rasputin, Protopopov, Trepov, Suxomlinov, Fredericks, Goremykin, Shcheglovitov, Kurlov, Maklakov, Shturmer. The overthrown autocracy is shown as nothing more than a broken puppet, with no substance to it, whilst the attitude of the peasant standing before it suggests bewilderment that it was not destroyed by the people long before.

Такъ вотъ что такой—императорскій тронъ,—

Предъ пугаломъ, значитъ, дрожали.

Зачѣмъ же проклятую стаю воронъ

Мы кровью своею питали?!

Перепечатка воспрещается фабрика А.Ф.ПОСТНОВА Москва т.л. 27-75

А.Ф.П.

National Funeral of Victims who Died for Freedom, 23 March 1917, in Petrograd

This view of the funeral procession of those who died in the February Revolution shows something of the solemnity of the occasion. This was well expressed by the Bolshevik Alexandra Kollontai, who wrote in *Pravda* the same day:

'Today is a solemn day of joy and of mourning. Today the eyes of the oppressed and deprived of the whole world are turned towards Russia, to this city where the heroic resolution of the workers and the downtrodden Russian peasantry has thrown off the yoke of tsarist autocracy.

'In saying farewell to the heroes who fell in the name of freedom, we will depart today from their graves imbued with firm resolution. The first step, the hardest step of the Revolution, has been taken. Tsarist autocracy, a decaying corpse upon a throne, has been committed to the earth.

'Today sees the completion of the first stage of the Revolution, the stage which consists of the destruction of the old. Now, comrades, let us hasten back to work! We must hurry, we must create the new! We must build a new, democratic, free Russia! Do not delay, comrades!'

Kollontai's article gives a clear indication that the Bolsheviks regarded the Revolution as far from complete, something she saw as only being achieved when 'the liberation of the working class' had been accomplished by a 'strong and stalwart' Bolshevik Party.

Всенародныя похороны жертвъ павшихъ за свободу
23-го Марта 1917 г. въ Петроградѣ.

The Workers' Marseillaise

Following the Revolution, the *Marseillaise* was adopted as an anthem of the new regime, with words that had been written by Peter Lavrov in 1875. The words of the first two verses and the refrain are redolent of the period:

Тебѣ отдыхъ — однѣ лишь могила!
Каждый день — недоимку готовь;
Царь-вампиръ изъ тебя тянетъ жилы;
Царь-вампиръ пьетъ народную кровь! (2 раза)
Ему нужны для войска солдаты:
Подай же сюда сыновей!
Ему нужны пиры да палаты!
Подавай ему кровь твоей!

Вставай, подымайся, рабочій народъ!
Вставай на враговъ, братъ голодный!
Раздайся, крикъ мести народной!
Впередъ! Впередъ! Впередъ!

Не довольно-ли вѣчнаго горя?
Встанемъ, братья, повсюду заразъ!
Отъ Днѣпра и до Бѣлаго моря,
И Поволжье, и дальній Кавказъ! (2 раза)
На воровъ, на собакъ — на богатыхъ!
Да на злого вампира-царя!
Бей, губи ихъ, злодѣевъ проклятыхъ!
Засвѣтись, лучшей жизни заря!

Вставай, подымайся, рабочій народъ!
Вставай на враговъ, братъ голодный!
Раздайся, крикъ мести народной!
Впередъ! Впередъ! Впередъ!

'Let us renounce the old world,
Let us shake its ashes from our feet!
We're enemies to the golden idols,
We detest the palaces of the Tsar!
We will go to suffering brothers,
We will go to hungry people;
With them we will send our curses to the evil-
  doers,
And call them to fight together with us:

'Arise, arise, working people!
Arise against the enemies, hungry brother!
Sound the cry of peoples' vengeance!
Forward! Forward! Forward!

'A greedy rack of rich men
Plunders your heavy work.
Gluttons grow fat on your sweat,
They tear the last piece from you.
Starve, for their feast!
Starve, for the stock exchange games
Where they sell conscience and honour,
And mock at you!'

Lavrov (1823–1900) was a member of the Narodnik Movement and editor of the revolutionary newspapers *People's Will* and *Forward*. He participated in the Paris Commune of 1871, and died in Paris in 1900.

РАБОЧАЯ МАРСЕЛЬЕЗА.

Отречемся отъ стараго міра,
Отряхнемъ его прахъ съ нашихъ ногъ!
Намъ враждебны златые кумиры,
Ненавистенъ намъ царскій чертогъ. (2 раза)
Мы пойдемъ въ ряды страждущихъ братій,
Мы къ голодному люду пойдемъ;
Съ нимъ пошлемъ мы злодѣямъ проклятья,
На борьбу мы его позовемъ:

Вставай, подымайся, рабочій народъ!
Вставай на враговъ, братъ голодный!
Раздайся, крикъ мести народной!
        Впередъ! Впередъ! Впередъ!

Богачи, кулаки жадной сворой
Расхищаютъ тяжелый твой трудъ.
Твоимъ потомъ жирѣютъ обжоры;
Твой послѣдній кусокъ они рвутъ. (2 раза)
Голодай чтобъ они пировали!
Голодай, чтобъ въ игрѣ биржевой
Они совѣсть и честь продавали,
Чтобъ ругались они надъ тобой!

Вставай, подымайся, рабочій народъ!

Вставай на враговъ, братъ голодный!
Раздайся, крикъ мести народной!
        Впередъ! Впередъ! Впередъ!

102

59

Kerensky with the 'Mother of the Revolution'

Alexander Kerensky (1881–1970) was born in Simbirsk, the same town as Lenin. He trained as a lawyer and was elected to the Duma of 1912 as a member of the Trudoviks, a moderate labour party. He played a prominent role in the February Revolution in 1917 and became Minister of Justice in the Provisional Government, whilst simultaneously serving as a vice-chairman of the Petrograd Soviet. In May 1917 he became Minister of War and the leading figure in the reconstituted socialist–liberal coalition government. Committed to continuing the unpopular war against Germany and Austria-Hungary, he launched the so-called 'Kerensky offensive' against the Central Powers. In July he became Prime Minister, and, following the attempted coup by General Kornilov in August, appointed himself Supreme Commander-in-Chief as well. It was thus easy for the Bolsheviks to portray him as a dictator and a Napoleon-in-waiting.

Kerensky's government had little popular support in Petrograd, enabling the Bolsheviks to overthrow it with remarkable ease in October 1917. Kerensky fled abroad, living in the United States from 1940 until his death in 1970. He is, however, buried in England, where his grave can be found, rather unexpectedly, at Putney Vale Cemetery in London.

The so-called 'Mother of the Revolution' was Catherine Breshkovsky (real name Yekaterina Konstantinovna Breshko-Breshkovskaya). She was born in 1844 and at the age of twenty-six she joined the anarchist followers of Bakunin in Kiev. Imprisoned in 1874, she was subsequently exiled to Siberia. After her release in 1896 she became one of the founders of the Socialist-Revolutionary Party, but had to escape abroad, first to Switzerland and then to the United States. She returned to Russia at the time of the 1905 Revolution, and was subsequently exiled to Siberia again. Released after the February Revolution in 1917, she became a member of Kerensky's government, but after the Bolshevik Revolution in October she was again forced to flee abroad. She died in Czechoslovakia in 1934.

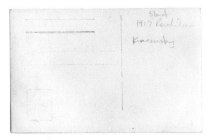

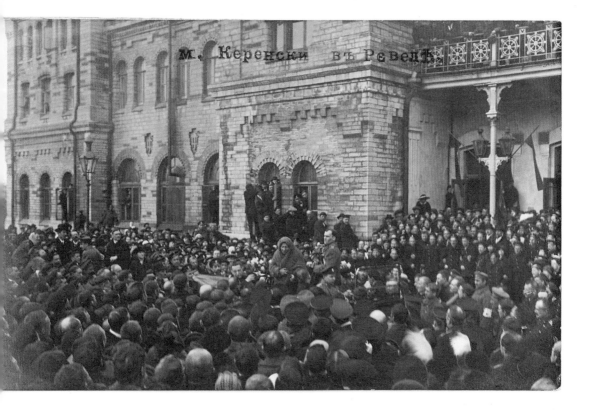

м. Керенски въ Ревелѣ.

61

Russian "Cossacks"
Reval 1917

Russian Cossacks, Reval, 1917

The situation in the Baltic provinces of the Russian Empire was very confused following the Revolution. The Estonians were determined to assert their independence, as were the Finns, Lithuanians and Latvians, whilst both Red and White Russians hoped that the Baltic provinces could be retained within Russia's boundaries. Foreign powers also had ambitions in the region. The Germans hoped that the Baltic States could be given a quasi-independence under German protection, whilst British naval forces based at Reval (Tallinn) were used to support both White attacks on Petrograd and Estonian attempts to gain their independence. Although Estonian independence was first declared in February 1918, this was not accepted by the Soviet government until the signing of the Treaty of Tartu in 1920.

The mounted forces described as Cossacks in this picture are wearing white armbands and may have formed part of the White Russian forces in the area.

63

Untitled

This view of troops preparing to defend a train is a reminder of the important role played by the railways during the Russian Revolution and especially during the Civil War that followed during 1918–20. Control of the railways enabled both the towns and cities to be supplied with food, and troops to be moved quickly from front to front. Both the Reds and the Whites made extensive use of armoured trains, of which the most famous was that used by Trotsky.

American Army landing at Vladivostock

Following the Russian Revolution, and the subsequent peace agreement between the Bolsheviks and Imperial Germany, a number of the Allied powers sent troops to Russia, ostensibly to prevent the vast quantities of supplies that they had sent to support Russia's war effort from falling into German hands. The Americans, who sent a force of over 7,000 men to Siberia, also hoped to rescue the troops of the Czechoslovak Legions who were using the Trans-Siberian Railway to reach Vladivostock, and then, it was hoped, go on to fight on the Western Front. President Woodrow Wilson also

hoped that this force would be sufficient to prevent any Japanese expansion into Siberia, and could support any Russian efforts at 'self-government or self-defense'.

The first American troops disembarked at Vladivostock between 15 and 21 August 1918, and the force remained in Siberia until April 1920. In that time they suffered relatively few casualties, but there were also a number of desertions by soldiers who stayed on in Russia for the rest of their lives.

American Army landing at Vladivostock. （其一）　米國陸軍浦塩斯德上陸ノ光景

ПОЧТОВАЯ КАРТОЧІ

Лондонъ Англіи

Miss I.E. Mckie
60 Prince of Wales Road
Battersea Park London SW. 11.
England

Untitled

This postcard was sent to the collector's mother and the interest lies in the message on the back, which dates from the period in early 1918 when many westerners were using the Trans-Siberian Railway to escape from revolutionary Russia. This could be a lengthy and hazardous journey. Florence Farmborough, a nurse who had served on the Russian front, took twenty-seven days to travel from Moscow to Vladivostock in a fourth-class carriage, which she thought had previously been used to transport convicts to Siberia. In her diary, she described her relief when the train eventually reached Vladivostock:

'It is wonderful that we are really here – at last! But what makes it all the more wonderful is that … in the harbour four large cruisers were anchored and one of them was flying the UNION JACK! Oh! The joy! The relief! The comfort! The security! Who will ever know all that this glorious flag symbolised for us travel-stained, weary refugees?'

April 3rd

In the train near Irkutsk

My dearest dear

Dont receive too great a shock
we are all in a special
wagon on our way to the
land of sunny dreams. We
left Omsk 4 days ago and
expect to be at least 2 weeks
in the train. Every thing is
so far is fine and the
children wonderfully little
trouble, they are born
travellers. Will write again
later on, I am just having
the time of my life. We have
one of my specials from Omsk
with us and my next things
we "going", the drama is perhaps
so cant write more Sil &
across Ura and Rives

69

Governor's House, Tobolsk

The royal family were imprisoned in the Governor's House in Tobolsk from August 1917 to April 1918 before they were sent to Ekaterinburg.

Astonishingly, members of the royal family were permitted to send messages to the outside world. This card was written by Grand Duchess Olga on 2 November 1917 to Peter Sergeivich Tolstoy in Odessa (at that time still under the control of the White forces). It reads, 'I send you my warmest thanks for your message and your good memories, O.'

Lenin Chats with V.M. Zagorsky, Secretary of the Moscow Committee of the Russian Communist Party, during the May Day Demonstration in Red Square, Moscow, May 1, 1919

Lenin's pose in this picture is very reminiscent of a description of him by the British socialist Harry Young, who heard him speak to the Fourth Congress of the Communist International (Comintern) in 1922:

'He spoke like a father or a "Dutch Uncle" addressing his rather wayward children. There was no oratory, no fireworks, no rhetoric. Instead he quietly and even humorously dealt with one point after another.'

V.M. Zagorsky (1883–1919) was born in Nizhni Novgorod, the son of Jewish parents. He became active in revolutionary movements in both Moscow and Petrograd, and was appointed Bolshevik party chief in Moscow in September 1918. He was assassinated by Left Socialist Revolutionaries in September 1919 and is buried in the Kremlin Wall. The town of Sergiyev Posad was renamed Zagorsk after him in 1930, but has now reverted to its former name.

Lenin in Red Square, 1 May 1919

This postcard purports to show Lenin talking to the
crowds in Red Square during the May Day parade, but its
composition suggests that it is a doctored photograph,
bringing together a picture of Lenin talking to close
supporters with one of a later parade or gathering. The
woman with her back to the camera to the left of Lenin
is his wife, Krupskaya.

Although the image dates from the early Soviet period,
this postcard is a later production.

Lenin Chats with the English Writer H.G. Wells in his Study in the Kremlin, Moscow, October 1920

Wells visited Russia for two weeks in the autumn of 1920 and wrote up his experiences in a book called *Russia in the Shadows*, published the same year. A believer in evolutionary socialism, Wells was unsympathetic towards Marxism, but thought that the Bolsheviks, in spite of their fanaticism, were honest and might well succeed in their aim of revitalizing Russia. He called Lenin 'The Dreamer in the Kremlin', and gave this revealing thumbnail sketch of his appearance:

'Lenin has a quick-changing brownish face with a lively smile and a habit (due perhaps to some defect in focusing) of screwing up one eye as he pauses in his talk; he is not very like the photographs you see of him because he is one of those people whose change of expression is more important than their features.'

Post Card

ONE
CENT
STAMP

SIGN THE ROLL CALL

Dear Friend:—The next two months will be the most crucial in the famine districts of Soviet Russia. Hundreds of thousands have already died and the little bread the more fortunate had is gone. Only one fourth of the starving have been helped. Fifteen million will die unless we all again give our limit immediately. Will you sign the ROLL CALL to prove that when the need was greatest you gave and so attested the solidarity of the workers? The ROLL CALL BOOK will be sent with shipments of food made in the next two months, to be deposited in Soviet Russia as a most honored document. Will it contain your name? Write the Friends of Soviet Russia, 201 West 13th Street, New York City, and tell them you want to SIGN UP.

Sincerely,

Dispensing food to the hungry.
A slice of bread is treasured more than you treasure a Sunday dinner

During the Russian Civil War there was large-scale famine in the country. As early as 1919 the American Relief Administration, headed by future president Herbert Hoover, offered food relief to Russia but this was rejected by the Bolsheviks, who feared the strings attached. Later, however, as the situation worsened, they changed their minds and allowed American aid into the country.

The Friends of Soviet Russia, who produced this postcard, operated quite separately from the ARA, which they attacked as having a political agenda in Russia, despite Hoover's assertion that 'Twenty million people are starving. Whatever their politics they shall be fed.' However, they too had a political agenda, as their official letterhead made quite clear:

'Our principle—We are making the working class appeal. Give not only to feed the starving but to save the Russian Workers' revolution. Give without imposing imperialistic and reactionary conditions as do Hoover and others.'

The sign on the side of the railway carriage reads 'Feeding Train no. 3. Kitchen'.

Dispensing food to the hungry. A slice of bread is treasured more than you treasure a Sunday dinner

V.I. Lenin, N.K. Krupskaya, and A.I. Elizarova with nephew Viktor and the daughter of the worker Vera. Gorki, 1922

This family view dates from when Lenin was in the sanatorium at Gorki (now Nizhni Novgorod) during the winter of 1921/22. Krupskaya sits next to Lenin. Anna Ilyinichna Ulyanova-Elizarova (1864–1935) was Lenin's older sister and herself an active revolutionary who was one of the managers of Surf, the Bolshevik publishing house, before it was closed down in 1914. In 1889 she married another revolutionary, the engineer Mark Elizarov (1863–1919), who later became the first Bolshevik Commissar for Transport after the October Revolution. When Lenin returned to Russia after the February Revolution he stayed at the Elizarov's flat on Shirokaya (now Lenin) Street in Petrograd; since 1927 this has been a museum. Viktor Ulyanov was the son of Lenin's younger brother, Dmitri. He later trained as an aircraft engineer in the 1930s and spent most of his life working in the defence industry dying in 1984, aged sixty-seven.

Lenin's Speech about the GOELRO Plan, 1922

This classic example of Socialist Realist art by L.A. Shmat'ko depicts Lenin's speech introducing the State Plan for the Electrification of Russia (GOELRO). Electrification was a key element in the Bolshevik plans to modernize Russia, Lenin even going so far as to state that Communism consisted of Socialism plus electrification.

GOELRO, developed under Lenin's direct leadership and approved by the VIII All-Russia Congress of Soviets in 1922, was the first long-term plan of development of a national economy based on the electrification of the country. Construction of thirty new large power stations having a general capacity of 1,750 thousand kilowatts was envisaged by the plan, which was completed ahead of schedule in 1931.

СО ЗНАМЕНЕМ ЛЕНИНА ПОБЕ-
ДИЛИ МЫ В БОЯХ ЗА ОКТЯБРЬ-
СКУЮ РЕВОЛЮЦИЮ. СО ЗНАМЕ-
НЕМ ЛЕНИНА ДОБИЛИСЬ МЫ
РЕШАЮЩИХ УСПЕХОВ В БОРЬБЕ
ЗА ПОБЕДУ СОЦИАЛИСТИЧЕСКОГО
СТРОИТЕЛЬСТВА. С ЭТИМ ЖЕ ЗНА-
МЕНЕМ ПОБЕДИМ И ПРОЛЕТАР-
СКОЙ РЕВОЛЮЦИИ ВО ВСЕМ МИ-
РЕ. ДА ЗДРАВСТВУЕТ ЛЕНИНИЗМ!
И. СТАЛИН.

5 в 4

И. В. СТАЛИН

Underground Work and Exile

This postcard seeks to promote the revolutionary past
of Joseph Stalin (real name Djugashvili), by depicting
Tsarist police photographs of him, a front page of the
revolutionary newspaper *The Baku Worker*, and views of
the Baku oil fields, where he was involved in agitation
amongst the workers in the early 1900s, and of Tiflis
(now Tblisi) where Stalin was born and grew up.

And God Rested

Much revolutionary propaganda was characterized by anti-clericalism, as the succeeding series of postcards produced by the 'Atheist at the Lathe' demonstrates.

The text is drawn from Genesis, 2: 2, and the quotation from Marx on the back reads, 'Criticism of religion is the beginning of any other criticism. Thus criticism of the heavens turns to criticism of the ground.'

Atheist Working at the Lathe was a magazine produced in Moscow in the 1920s. The artist was Dmitry Moor (Orlov) (1883–1946).

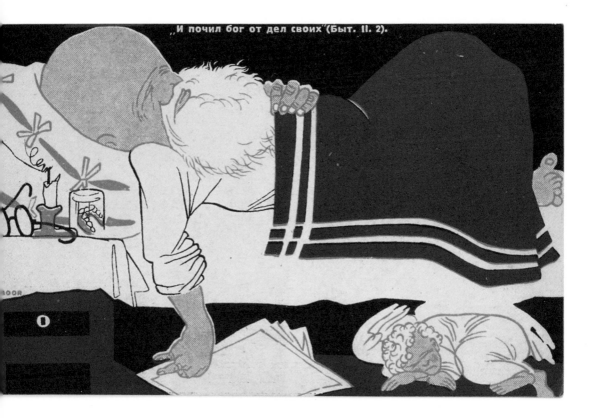

„И почил бог от дел своих"(Быт. II. 2).

God Writes his Memoirs

Another postcard from 'Atheist at the Lathe'. God is shown beginning to write the Bible (the text begins, 'On the first day I created the sky …').

The commentary by 'Atheist' on the back of the postcard reads, 'Priests insist that the concept of God is naturally within him. Well, it means that man is a slave of nature. It is a lie. If you bring up your son without the priest's lie, he will grow up as a free and strong worker for socialism.'

Бог пишет свои воспоминания—

Let there be Light!

In this cartoon the Biblical quotation is from Genesis 1: 3. The quotation on the back is from Lenin and reads, They said before "Each one for himself and God for all". But how much sorrow have we had? We say "One for all, and we will do without God one way or another".'

Don't Eat the Apples! I Shall Eat Them.

The reference is clearly to the story of Adam and the Tree of Knowledge. 'Atheist' contrasts God's order with the ironic comment by Voltaire, 'My friend, if you were the landowner and were afraid that the unbridled crowd were going to plunder you, you would understand what an important role the kind God plays for all of us. If God does not exist, he should be invented.'

— Яблочков не кушать: я сам буду их есть.

Untitled

This portrait of Lenin as a child was widely disseminated after the Revolution and was prominently displayed in schools, where children were taught that they should aspire to be as 'perfect' as the young Lenin supposedly had been. Thus Lenin became the icon of the new orthodoxy.